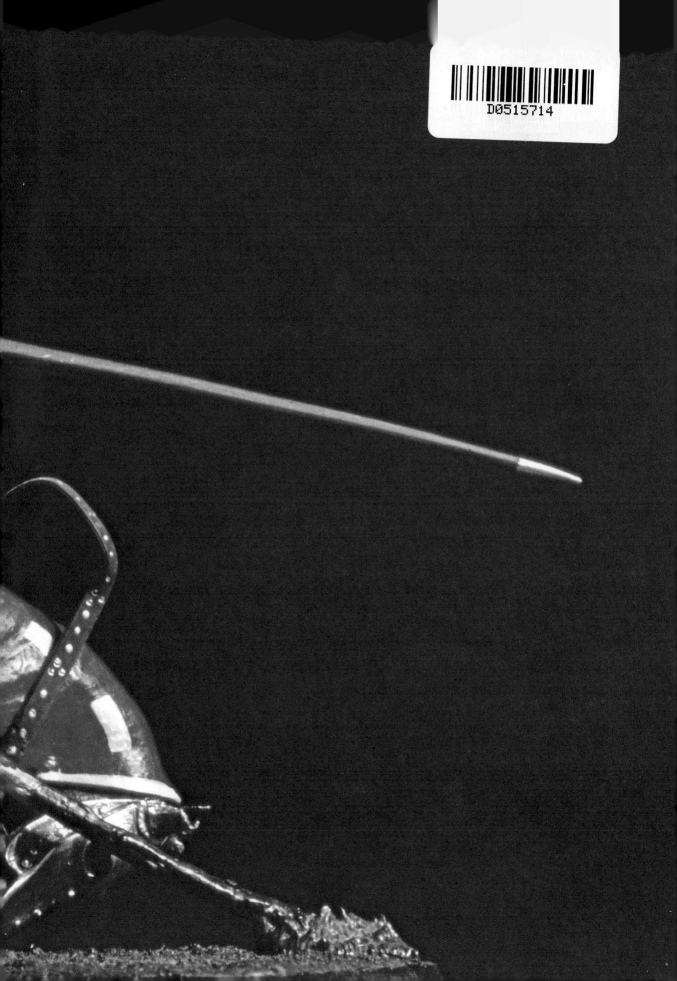

D0515714

Thanks for
everything—

Steve Szyszko

Roger Hoobema

John Sullivan

aaron smith

Matt
Nottingham

Paul Chesnutt

Ty Coon

Paul Ledford

Model Soldiers
IN COLOR
Roy Dilley

octopus

CONTENTS

A knight's charge is halted by stakes at Agincourt (endpapers); he wears a composite plate and mail armour. (WMH Models) The diorama (title page) shows a Napoleonic infantryman snapshooting from the cover of stone walls. (David Buffrey) Contrasting methods of transport are depicted in an entertaining World War I scene (left). (David Catley) (The names in brackets refer to the modellers.)

INTRODUCTION

Only a decade or so ago 'model' soldiers were thought of by many people as 'toy' soldiers and were hardly ever considered to be anything other than colourful playthings. Collection of such pieces by adults might indeed have been looked upon with some degree of suspicion as showing a great degree of eccentricity. These views, reinforced by the undoubted fact that most military figures were produced commercially as toys, tended to run down the hobby of military-figure collecting. Therefore collectors, for the most part, enjoyed their pastime in isolation with only the occasional press article, sometimes rather patronizing, to publicize the fact that there might be others with similar interests.

The case today is quite different, with enthusiasts the world over. Their hobby involves not just collecting military miniatures, but painting, converting and building them from scratch. These people are often banded together in societies and clubs, supported by a sizeable industry which turns out basic materials, figures, accessories and equipment of all kinds. They are also backed up by a constant flow of reference data, books, prints, cards, photographs and the like. Standards of work achieved by many of its foremost practitioners have raised military modelling to a true art form, widely acclaimed and respected.

Although model soldiers have been the subject of serious collecting interest only in comparatively recent times, they have had, in some form or another, a history of several thousand years. Representations in miniature of fighting men have been found in the tombs of Egyptian warriors, such as Prince Emsah who was buried at Assiut in Upper Egypt around 2000 BC. The Greeks and Romans cast little bronze and lead warriors as playthings or votary objects; while in the Middle Ages and the Renaissance military figures in wood, leather, metal, even stone, were made for the children of the rich. During the 16th, 17th and 18th centuries many model soldiers, some organized as complete armies and often cast in precious metals, silver and gold, brightened the childhoods of princes and nobles. Few now survive and it is probable that most of

A group of American staff officers in Vietnam (right) making plans beside a tracked armoured command vehicle. (D. Skinner)

them, melted down, went to finance the activities of real armies – perhaps not an altogether unfitting end. Certainly, a priceless collection given to Louis XIII of France by his mother was sold by Louis XIV for its silver content.

The 18th century saw the production of paper soldiers – souvenir sheets which could be backed onto cardboard and used as toys. They were cheap and popular and widely available. It was mass production of metal figures, the flat two-dimensional *zinnfiguren* designed by German master-engravers centred on the city of Nuremberg, that

brought down the cost, made model soldiers available to a much wider market, and laid the foundations for the 'tin soldier' tradition. The 19th century saw the introduction of *ronde bosse* – fully modelled types – along with the continuing expansion of the flat ranges and, in the closing years, the invention of hollow-cast techniques. This meant that model

Types from the ancient world are the subjects of these exquisite flats (above). (Jim Woodley) A Roman gladiator (right) in before and after aspects shows how deft painting can bring a model to life. (John Tassel)

could be manufactured in quantities and at prices that brought them within the reach of the average family budget. These pieces, marshalled on lawn, carpet or table top by their youthful generals, were well designed and adequately painted by commercial standards; they have today acquired the status of antiques and are sought by collectors.

Because of the metal shortage after World War I and the fact that the Germans had been forbidden under the Versailles Treaty from making military toys, soldier modelling and collecting fell off. Just before World War II some enthusiasts, who not only collected but also altered or 'converted' these commercially produced items to other types and positions, began to band together, giving one another mutual support and providing for an interchange of ideas and techniques. The British Model Soldier Society, the oldest of these groups, was formed in 1935. After the war, production of hollow-cast metal figures was gradually resumed but never quite reached the range and diversity achieved during the inter-war period. With the introduc-

tion of suitable plastics, together with stringent regulations prohibiting the use of certain materials, principally lead, in the manufacture of toys, production ceased for all practical purposes in about 1966.

However, sculptors and artists, many of great distinction, have applied their talents to the design of specialized 'connoisseur' figures and equipment intended for the collector market – that is, not as toys. These figures, cast or moulded in white metal or hard plastics and sold frequently as kits for assembly by the modeller, form much of the basic material for today's enthusiasts. Aids to modelling such as sheet, strip and rod plastic, self-hardening resins and putty, miniature tools of all kinds, adhesives and paints have all made significant advances in recent years, giving even more scope for the development of skills and advanced techniques. Perhaps most important is the sense of realism in presentation which has become firmly established. Men, animals, machines and equipment are now depicted in their proper environments, rather than just as individual pieces each on its own base.

ANCIENT WORLD

Fighting in early days was very much a hand-to-hand affair. Some protection was given by basic weapons and shields or light armour such as that developed by the Romans, but much depended on a man's own personal skills and the bravery of his comrades, typified by these Anglo-Saxon warriors (*below*). (J. MacOmish)

Better organized than any other in the ancient world, the Roman army had its main strength in mighty legions, comprised of foot soldiers whose duties included road and fort building as well as fighting, ceremonial and peacekeeping activities. Renowned for an ability to march great distances, legionaries carried their weapons and other gear slung over their shoulders or tied to long poles. One of these soldiers is modelled completely laden (*top left*), and it is easy to understand from this fine piece

w the legion nickname 'Marius's Mules' arose.
. Wilcox)

When fighting at close quarters, the Roman
fantryman stabbed upwards at his opponent from
e shelter of his deep cylindrical shield, an effective
chnique which presented a solid barrier to any
emy and carried the legions victoriously to the
er-expanding frontiers of the then known world.
this model (*below left*) the protection given by the
ield is well illustrated, together with the complex

helmet and the segmented iron-strip body armour.
(Terry Smith)

The Roman army also contained cavalry and
mounted infantry units who worked and fought
alongside the legions and provided many of the men
for garrison, patrol, policing and escort duties as
well as baggage and food convoy guards. The scenic
group (*below*) depicts a cavalryman of an auxiliary
unit contemplating the snow-covered remains of a
former enemy left to die on the field. (P. Wilcox)

Many of Rome's early rivals were formidable and included the Carthaginian Empire, whose power under the famous general Hannibal came close to destroying the Roman state. Hannibal's army included a number of elephants which carried wooden towers on their backs filled with javelin throwers and archers, a splendid example of moving artillery (*left*). The power and majesty of these living castles (which caused great consternation in the Roman ranks, until methods were worked out to deal with them) is strikingly portrayed here to a scale of 9.5 mm to .304 mm ($\frac{3}{8}$ in to 1 ft), a standard model-soldier scale recognized internationally. (P. Wilcox)

Always aware of the threat of being overthrown or assassinated, the rulers of Rome raised an elite personal protection unit known as the Praetorian Guard. This select force played an important, sometimes decisive role in Roman political affairs, gaining a rather unsavoury reputation in the process. This imposingly dressed Praetorian officer (*right*), with his air of ruthless efficiency, sums up the Roman military command during the period of that civilization. (P. Wilcox)

The figure of a mounted Scythian archer is posed (*below*) in a scenic setting. The standards of excellence achieved in the creation and finish of these models reveal the artist's skill. (John Tassel)

Typical of the nomadic peoples who roamed across the steppes of Asia more than two thousand years ago were the Scythians. Their way of life enabled them, by using the sturdy steppe ponies for riding and load-carrying, to survive and flourish in vast areas that would not support farming settlement. They fought with or against most of the established nations of their period and enjoyed great success in their tactics which were based on the horse archers. These swift-moving marksmen could strike at a target, inflicting physical injury and damage to morale, and dart quickly back out of reach.

Dressed in clothes made from leather, felt and wool, multi-coloured and beautifully embroidered, the Scythians and their well-equipped ponies make ideal model subjects as can be seen in the picture (*below*) which shows a metal miniature of a horse archer turning in the saddle to discharge his missiles. (P. Wilcox)

More than a thousand years after the slow decline of Scythian cultures, the coastlines of western Europe and the Mediterranean were occasionally attacked and eventually settled by a seafaring race from Scandinavia. Brave warriors who fought on foot with axe, spear and sword, the Vikings, as they were known, had developed a type of vessel, the longship, in which they sailed or rowed astonishing distances for those days. It is said that they even reached the shores of North America, establishing a colony there.

Some impression of Viking strength and vitality is conveyed by this magnificent large-scale model (*right*). Cast in white metal and then painted with stunning effect, the model is an excellent example of the way in which careful choice of paints and technique, in the rendering of different textures such as steel and cloth, contribute to the realism of the piece. (D. Maskell)

wo more examples of warriors from ancient times
e a Syrian auxiliary of the Roman army (*left*) and
 Ta-ta nomad from central Asia (*above*) with his
eavily loaded pack camel. (P. Wilcox) Both these
gures are in standard scale but so carefully have
ey been modelled and painted that they lose little
` their effect even when, as in these photographs,
ey are magnified to several times their actual size.
he materials used in the construction of these
eautiful pieces include white metal (an alloy of
lead, antimony and tin), hard and soft plastics, wire,
plaster, sheet brass and anything else that can
possibly give the impression of the necessary textures. Similarly, the type of paint which produces
the best results on each detail is the one used, and
quite often several different kinds are applied to the
one miniature. In practising this art form the aim is
to get the best degree of realism conveyed by
accuracy of shape, proportion and balance in figure,
pose and presentation.

MEDIEVAL TIMES

The Middle Ages saw developments in defensive architecture, improvements in weaponry, the progression from helm and mail to complete suits of plate armour and, most strikingly, the evolution of heraldic systems of identification. In the chess set (*below*) medieval colour is deftly caught. (Historex)

Japanese warriors presented an impression as brilliant as that seen in Europe, as these models amply illustrate (*above* by Ray Lamb and *right* by Paul Campen). It was not, of course, only in Europe that changes were taking place in military thought, in the development of weapons and armour and in the increasing use of badges and symbols for identification of men and armies. In many ways these matters were going forward much more quickly in the kingdoms and empires of the Eastern world. Certainly the influence of the Saracens on the Crusaders was very strong and the crusading knights brought these ideas back to the West. A similar feudal system existed in Japan. There were significant advances in Japan in the techniques of tempering, working and decorating metals to make them beautiful and tough, as well as useful. Much use was made of wood and padding in Japanese composite armours which were lacquered, painted and often worn with undergarments in bright colours and intricate patterns.

Much of the colour associated with the Middle Ages comes from the use of heraldic arms and related items, such as fur and coloured cloth, not only on battle gear but also on civilian dress. A 13th-century knight (*below*) shows a typical use of colourful heraldry on his shield, surcoat and horse trappings. Also of interest are the predominantly mail armour, the 'great helm', and the axe, carried instead of the more usual lance. (T. Nappin)

Representing a crossbowman from a hundred or so years later, the nicely finished figure (*below right*) is also armed with a sword and protected with a *chapeau de fer* steel cap, mail hood, cape and shirt and odd plates of steel at his waist and knee. The crossbow discharged a bolt with a great deal of power, though it was slower to load than the longbow. (John Tassel)

As a ready means of identifying individuals in the heat of battle, at tournaments and courtly gatherings, heraldry served an obvious purpose. In an age

when even the highest born were not very good at the arts of reading and writing, heraldic devices on seals were commonly used as signatures on documents or as marks of ownership on items of property. The grants of arms or, as in the beginning of the system, taking them on without asking the sovereign or any other authority, meant that in the course of time there were too many devices. Since most arms were hereditary, and identified large families and their particular relationships, any new arms were shown by marks of 'difference' on the original arms. So complex became these devices, particularly with families who had been joined by marriage, that a need for a specialist arose, someone who could memorize the many designs, their differences and combinations. These experts were known as heralds and their duties included communication between opposing forces and arbitration, as well as keeping a register of the family trees and coats of arms of the nobles.

An attacking knight, fully armoured, having weathered the storm of arrows and broken into his enemy's line, could then create havoc amongst lightly protected archers and foot-soldiers. Their only hope lay in a lucky blow which might bring the knight to the ground where the weight of his gear would make it impossible for him to move. He could then be killed or, more likely, compelled to yield for ransom. Among the more lowly soldiers with no remote possibility of exchanging their lives for ransom, defeat in battle all too often meant a quick death unless they were lucky and a plea for quarter met with a favourable response. This dramatic scene (*left*) depicts an incident during the battle of Agincourt (1415) and captures the sadness of such a situation. (M. Perry)

Typical of foot-sodliers at the close of medieval times (1500) is this billman (*above*), armed with sword, little round buckler and deadly polearm, known as the bill, a weapon in which axe, spear and hook are combined in the one curiously shaped blade. With light armour protecting only his more vital points, knees and midriff, he is suitably equipped to tackle mounted or dismounted opponents, trusting in his skill at arms and agility. (W. Ganley)

HORSE AND MUSKET

This was an era lasting more than three hundred years, in which firearms gradually became more reliable and effective until they all but dominated the battlefield, reducing the polearm eventually to a mere symbol. The scenic group (*below*) shows troops praying before going into action in the English Civil War. (D. Catley)

At the beginning of the 16th century elaborate civilian-type dress was worn by fighting men, with puffed and slashed garments and plumed headgear, as can be seen in this merry swordsman (*above*), representative of the Landsknecht-type warrior. (K. Lazenbury)

Less flamboyant but with a distinct air of purpose and efficiency, the Hungarian hussar (*right*) is as he would have looked in about the year 1600. (John MacOmish)

Regiments of light horse were raised at this time in Hungary by levying one man from every 20 families, the word *hussa* meaning a 'twentieth man', subsequently changed to 'hussar'. This system resulted in troops who became the national cavalry of Hungary and adopted a distinctive style of dress with fur cap and cloak, braided tunic and soft leather boots. So successful did they become that other countries raised similar units, adopting at the same time the hussar dress which, with national modifications, remained typical of this type of cavalry in armies until comparatively recent times. The functions of light cavalry were concerned with scouting, patrolling, escort duties, harassment and exploitation of any weaknesses in the enemy and chasing retreating or routed forces. Shock action was not their prime battle task, although they could be very useful in charging disorganized formations. Following the Hungarian tradition, small, sturdy men, mounted on light, active horses, were preferred in hussar regiments.

A Zieten hussar of Frederick the Great's time (1740–86) is depicted in a piece (*above right*) which clearly illustrates the ornate ceremonial uniforms of these elite light cavalrymen. The cost of such outfits must even in those days have been enormous, both to provide and to maintain them properly. Well proportioned and balanced, the figure was cast from an original design by the sculptor Tim Richards. Connoisseur pieces of this kind are generally supplied in the form of unpainted castings which need to be assembled, and they require careful finishing to achieve their full effect. (A. Tatman)

Midway through the 18th century Britain and France were locked in combat in the densely wooded areas of the American-Canadian borderlands as part of their worldwide struggle in the Seven Years' War. A French infantryman of about 1736 (*above left*) is armed and equipped in a style that lasted throughout the fighting. This figure is another example of a superbly designed creation, every detail clearly engraved and meticulously finished to a high level of historical accuracy. (John Tassel)

Another Prussian hussar (*right*), a trumpeter in service uniform (1770), is posed upon an interesting little base made from a slice of log with some groundwork added and a neatly lettered, etched brass nameplate. Even such a simple impression of an environment adds realism and impact to the presentation. (Kevin Brown)

During the Seven Years' War both sides made use of Red Indians as allies, and the fighting was very savage. European troops, used to strictly drilled tactical manoeuvring, were at a great disadvantage compared with Indians and woodsmen who knew the country, and so were especially vulnerable to ambush. In 1755 a British column commanded by General Braddock was surprised and shattered in an ambush in thick forest along the Monongahela River by a mixed force of French and Indians. Only about a third of nearly 1,400 men came through the action unharmed on the British side. In a scenic piece (*overleaf*), the modeller has re-created a moment from the action, and captures some of the atmosphere of that fierce encounter in the North American wilderness. (David Hunter)

THE ART OF MILITARY MODELLING

An acceptable definition of military modelling is 'the representation in miniature of fighting men, their dress, weaponry, equipment, auxiliaries and supporters'. The hobby can conveniently be classified into two main categories: collecting and modelling. The first implies the acquisition of pieces upon which the collector carries out no work, except perhaps simple assembly and painting. The second is either the actual creation of miniatures by a 'scratchbuilding' process, or the alteration of existing models by means of conversion. There are many enthusiasts whose pursuit of the hobby embraces both its aspects, thus taking advantage of commercially produced items and at the same time allowing full scope for creativity.

Scratchbuilding describes the construction of a piece completely from scratch; its conception, design and execution being carried out by the modeller using basic materials. Conversion is the term used for the process of changing a manufactured model by altering its pose, repainting it to represent some other type, or completely reshaping it, with or without the addition of parts.

BACKGROUND KNOWLEDGE

Both modelling categories involve the art of shaping and painting the basic materials to convey an impression of real people, animals, vehicles etc., and this depends upon the acquisition of skills in handling tools and materials, and on the use of these skills with flair and originality. As with most things, practice and experience lead to the development of characteristic styles and the best technique. But although the techniques can be learnt with practice, the end result will not be interesting unless you use your imagination. The presentation needs to be just that little bit different. So many really first-class figures and assembly kits are available today that the temptation just to put them together or paint them 'as is' is powerful. However, a little imagination will render them unique.

Clearly, to be effective in the art of military modelling the modeller needs to gain some knowledge of human and animal anatomy and the clothing and weaponry relative to a particular soldier's rank. It is also important to accumulate as much technical information about military machinery and equipment as possible. By providing the source material for such knowledge, the collection of books, pictures, actual items of dress and so on can also become a valuable and enjoyable aspect of the hobby, together with visits to military displays, museums, battle sites and libraries. Only by soaking up a great deal of information can the modeller get the essential 'feel' for his subject. Most of the acknowledged masters of the art are also extremely knowledgeable about the real-life backgrounds of their subjects.

SCENIC SETTINGS

The recent development of military modelling has seen a significant trend towards the use of scenic settings in which models are shown to

eater advantage. Just as real soldiers exist in
a environment, so models of them can be
ade more effective by being placed in
iniature scenes which help to give a lifelike
mpression of some particular incident. The
eation of these scenes is regarded as one of the
ost attractive aspects of the art. If the painter
a picture can persuade the viewer of his work
by means of colours applied to a flat surface –
at he is looking at solid forms, various
xtures and real distances, then the modeller
ust set out his three-dimensional picture with
e same intention. The more skilfully
mposition, materials, techniques and
agination are combined, the more effective
comes the illusion of reality. Natural
bstances such as sand, rock fragments, mosses
all kinds, seedlings, twigs and dried grasses,
well as artificial aids like model railway
rass' matting, cast plaster mouldings of
ildings, walls and pillars, printed cardboard
presenting stone and brickwork, wood veneers
d strip can help the artist in the construction
convincing settings.

We know that we are only looking at
dments of painted metal and plastic, yet we
n smell horses, hear the trumpets and feel the
bre cuts. Of course, not all modellers,
rticularly those new to the art, can achieve
this, but the fun is in trying.

BJECT MATTER

is important to be aware that military
odelling is not just concerned with 'blood and
thunder' subjects. In real life only a small
proportion of a soldier's time is spent in action.
Just as much subject material for interesting
modelling can be found in the situations of
everyday life in town or barracks, on the parade
ground, or in 'out-of-action' campaign
incidents; nor need humour be neglected in the
consideration of suitable material. There are also
purely informative types of models. These are
concerned with the detail of uniform and
equipment, or the accurate representation of
vehicles and artillery pieces. Mention must also
be made of the differences in scale, which mean
that, in a manageable area, you can achieve
impeccable detail on a large statuette, typified
by Dave Whitbread's Red Indian figures (see
page 50), and at the other extreme the
impression of the action taking place over a
large area of country, as in the exquisite
$\frac{1}{60}$th scale dioramic settings of Edward Suren, or
the even smaller scale dioramas depicting
phases of the Battle of Waterloo, which were
made in the last century by Captain Siborne.

The scope is vast; soldiers, tanks, and guns
are obvious military subjects, but there is much
more in the animal kingdom and an enormous
variety of service, commercial, private and
agricultural vehicles and machines, which at
some point or another, are connected with a
soldier's life. Because of its infinite source of
subject material, military modelling, with its
challenges to ingenuity and imagination,
provides an ideal aesthetic and recreational
pastime.

NAPOLEONIC WARS

Although, properly speaking, the Napoleonic Wars fall firmly into the horse-and-musket era, the long drawn-out period of the wars against republican and imperial France has come to occupy a special position for military model makers. Its colourful uniforms, variety of types, and the abundance of relevant figures and kits available to collectors make it a favourite theme. This lively group of British soldiers (*below*), produced in 80-mm (3-in) scale, illustrates a scene from the battle of Famars (1793). (DEK Models)

Soldiering does not consist entirely of fighting and some of its less serious aspects, involving ceremonies, games or music, provide rich scope for interesting, or even amusing miniatures. Humour should not be ignored when a model subject is being considered, for it will often serve to make a stronger impact than more straightforward treatment might produce. The large-scale figure (*above*) is an excellent instance where humorous handling has given a forceful impression of a lighter moment on active service. This musically inclined French hussar is clad in the uniform worn during the campaign in the Peninsular (1808–14) and is clearly getting a great amount of pleasure from his singing and playing. (D. Whitbread)

Also represented in a relaxed attitude, this French mounted scout (*left*) has improved his army rations by doing a little hunting, judging by the plump rabbit slung from his saddle. Delightful treatment of the horse and the simple groundwork contribute to the appeal of this lively and extremely attractive presentation. (Kevin Brown)

An attractive inn facade provides support for the French figures in this village scene (*above right*). Every detail of construction has been observed and faithfully reproduced, such features as the shutters, pump, trough and swinging sign being particularly well done. Work like this inspires keen admiration in model makers of all degrees of ability, not least among competition judges, who look for and reward such detail and skill. (Mick Jewell)

Painstaking attention to detail is also apparent in the magnificent $\frac{1}{12}$th scale figure of a trumpeter in the Imperial Guard Horse Grenadiers of 1810 (*left*). The intention in this type of figure is to offer as complete an impression as possible of every feature of a soldier's uniform at a specific time. Buckles, buttons, cords and lace are shown with great clarity and the figure's general attitude indicates the pride of serving in an elite corps. (B. Harris)

The third picture (*below right*) shows the figure of a Voltigeur or skirmisher of the 29th Infantry at the battle of Wagram, 1809. This rear view shows the soldier's short sabre or *briquet*, cooking pan and bundle of sticks for use in lighting a fire. (B. Harris)

There is no doubt that the more complex type of scenic setting, or diorama as it has come to be known among modellers (although the term strictly applied refers to a cased presentation meant for viewing from one direction only), has become much more popular in recent years. It makes sense that since real people exist in an environment, then models of them will be more realistic and convincing if displayed in or on a setting that suggests an actual location. Such a setting can often provide a reason for a figure or group to be carrying out a particular activity or assuming a certain posture. In presentations that tell a story or establish a precise location, it is really necessary to research the actual area so that errors in vegetation, soil colour, architectural features and so on can be avoided in the model. The value of accurate research cannot be overemphasized.

Much of Britain's success in the Napoleonic Wars was due to a superiority at sea which meant that invasion could be prevented, trade protected and troops easily transported wherever they might be needed. Raids and combined operations were carried out by troops, marines and sailors, often using the boat from a warship (*below*). Points to note on this model are the gun and crew positioned in the bows, and the officers and drummer in the stern. (A. Robinson)

It must be remembered that Napoleon's power was largely land-based, relying on the huge French armies which were increased in size by the forces of allied states and nations, many of whom had been former opponents. These armies meant that the greater part of Europe was under French domination. Only the British Isles, shielded from attack, were able to provide significant resistance and bolster the few countries that did continue to oppose efforts by Napoleon to bring them under the French flag.

After Trafalgar, British ships were able to sail the oceans unthreatened by enemy vessels, which meant that the movement of British troops was relatively easy and effective in stopping any seaborne transportation of enemy troops. The fleet could cover the landing of troops, the supplies of stores and other necessities, and taking the troops out

again if necessary. The French cavalry arm, r organized in 1791 with the rest of the servic developed after a poor start into a most powerf force, which exerted a decisive influence on the mar important battles by which Napoleon's empire w expanded. The French had a balanced force for mc of this period with a fair proportion of lig horseman, hussars, chasseurs and lancers (the lig cavalry). It was the heavy cavalry, however, wl delivered the shock action in battle; a mobi battering ram of men and horses that, used at t right moment, was capable of breaking up t enemy's ranks and dealing one at a time with t disorganized mob which was usually produced eve among steady, experienced soldiers as the result such an attack. Napoleon himself was of the opinic that 'in the heavy cavalry . . . the art and science of t mounted man is exemplified to the highest orde and that the cuirassiers were of greater value tha any other type of cavalry. These heavy troops their name implies, were equipped with back ar breast armour as, after 1810, were two regiments carabiniers – elite cavalrymen, similar to the hor grenadiers, who had previously worn plain coats ar tall bearskin caps. The carabinier trumpeter (*right*) wearing this fur cap and his coat is of the regimen facing colour, still the custom for trumpeters durir that period. (K. Northrop)

The Imperial Guard of Napoleon I was in effect an army within an army, having its own cavalry, infantry, artillery and other supporting arms and services. It was subdivided into Old, Middle and Young Guards, each category having its own status depending on the length of service and/or the method of recruitment. Thus the 'old guard' were veterans of many years' service in the Line before entering a Guard unit; the 'young guard' were the pick of the enrolled men or conscripts; and the 'middle guard' were fusiliers and instruction battalions for the most part, a rough description but basically correct. Among the Emperor's favourite units of the Guard were the squadrons of Chasseurs à Cheval, light cavalry specializing in reconnaissance and escort duties. Their uniforms were predominantly green in colour and with a definite hussar cut. Modelled in 25-mm (1-in) scale, the 2nd Chasseurs à Cheval of the Guard, a short-lived formation, are shown at the charge (*right*), with standard bearer and trumpeter. Figures in this scale are commonly used for wargames but at their best incorporate much engraved detail which can be picked out with care in painting, to result in pieces of connoisseur quality. (P. Wilson)

This little scene (*below*) presents us with the

nperor himself, taking a nap with Marengo, his
ourite charger, cropping the grass at his side.
apoleon is wearing his familiar grey overcoat and
e boots to which he gave his name, and by his
air rest his distinctive hat and sword. This
arming example of the modeller's art has de-
rvedly won international acclaim in a number of
portant competitions and displays. (Alan
aselup)

A grenadier colour-sergeant in the British 44th
oot, the East Essex Regiment (*right*), is a member
a fine English corps which not only served with
eat distinction in the Peninsular, capturing the
gle of the French 62nd Line Regiment at Salam-
ca, but also stood in those stubborn squares at
aterloo, standing off attack after attack, and
ally destroying forever Napoleon's hopes of re-
tablishing his empire. The sergeant wears rank
signia on both sleeves; that on the right shows his
ecial status as a colour-guard. Other items of his
nk are the half pike over his shoulder, the crimson
sh with wide stripe of facing colour, and the sword
on his left hip. Such men were the backbone of the
rvice, steady and reliable in peace and in war,
en upholders of regimental honour and tradition
d setting high standards to be aimed at by all. (A.
. Sturgeon)

COLONIAL BATTLES

The 19th century was essentially a time of expansion, with powerful countries seeking markets for the products of their developing industrial systems, newly established nations pushing for their place in the sun, and more and more areas of the world opening up to exploration and exploitation. Colonization, friendly or otherwise, could seldom be practised without friction which needed to be contained, by force in extreme cases. Armies mainly recruited from native populations helped colonial powers to resist attack from without and contain any rebellion within their possessions. Such was the magnificent Indian Army which, commanded by European and native officers, helped a comparatively small British presence to keep the peace in the entire sub-continent. This splendid group (*left*) makes use of basic 80-mm (3-in) figures designed by Sid Horton. It is an example of the spirit of the Indian Army in which mutual respect welded together different nationalities into a powerful fighting force. (J. Hearn)

A great hunger to possess and work land of th
own sent thousands of settlers westwards across
prairies of North America from the 1840s onwar
in another kind of colonial expansion. Inevitabl
these settlers aroused the anger of Red Indian trib
who saw their traditional hunting grounds overr
and the animals upon which their economy v
based either killed or driven off. The position v
not improved by discoveries of gold and oth
minerals, which attracted fortune seekers. N
unnaturally, Indian anxieties sometimes explod
into violent action. This required some move on
part of the US Government – protection for
continuing inflow of settlers and permanent ba
from which to exercise control over the vast are
that were involved. Of course, it fell to the lot of
US Army to meet all these requirements. Forts w
established all over the western plains garrisoned
a fairly small regular army, in some cases increas
in size by locally raised volunteer units, oft
undisciplined and poorly led. No such complai
could be levelled against the regulars, typified
the craggy cavalry NCO in about 1860 (abou
modelled in 90-mm (3.5-in) scale, and the $\frac{1}{9}$th sc
'buffalo soldier' as the Indians called negro troc
(left). (Realmodels; Dave Whitbread)

Movement westward was severely curtailed
the outbreak of civil war between the states, invo
ing soldiers such as this Confederate colour bea
(right). (David Hunter)

When Columbus 'discovered' America there were, it is estimated, more than 2,000 tribes of Indians living there, totalling nearly one million people. Each community rarely consisted of more than 150 people, but they were spread across the whole continent. Indians lived by hunting, fishing and, in certain cases, primitive agriculture. There was much travelling about on trading, hunting and warlike expeditions, and journeys of many hundreds of kilometres were not unusual.

On the plains, the first Spanish explorers striking up from Mexico released some horses and these animals multiplied very quickly, to form huge herds of wild mustangs. The Indians in those parts learned to catch and train the horses for riding, and soon became the best light cavalry ever seen. It was principally these mounted tribes who were encountered by the 19th-century settlers as they moved westward. Had the tribes been larger or banded together against the invaders they may have been more successful in halting the flow, but they were proud and independent and had in the end to give way to the white man. While it lasted, however, Red Indian resistance was stubborn and bitter.

The war dress of chiefs and warriors was striking and, added to their painted features, presented a sight to chill all but the very stoutest hearts. Some idea of the effects achieved can be gained from these wonderful large-scale models of a Sioux chieftain (*left*) and a Hidatsa dog soldier (*right*). Contributing to the impact of these pieces are the carefully modelled physical details, the poses, the authentic well-researched features of clothing and weapon, and the use of 'natural' materials. For instance, the chief's headdress is made of real feathers, his trousers from soft tanned leather, his breechclout from cloth, his arm ornaments from quills and beads and his short carbine from metal and wood. The same attention has been paid to the model of the dog soldier in which a high degree of ingenuity combined with the 'right' materials, have produced a figure of great power and conviction. (David Whitbread)

At the height of British rule in India, the Raj, as it was known, had at its disposal not only the highly trained Indian Army but also, in difficult times, the forces of various princely states whose rulers, owing allegiance to the Crown though not part of British India, would offer their services. This man was a native officer of the 3rd Skinner's Horse (*left*), a cavalry regiment of the Indian Army. Every detail of the gorgeous uniform is clearly revealed in a model of outstanding merit, even the intricate Kashmir embroidery on the hanging end of the sash or cummerbund, and the delicate gold lace on the front panel of the long coat or kurta. (J. Runnicles)

The camel sowar or trooper (*right*) is a member of the Bikanir Ganga Risala, a famous regiment in the army of a princely state situated in the dry regions of western India. This is a 77-mm (3-in) scale model. (J. Wilmshurst)

In the third picture (*below*) the locale is Africa where, during the Sudan War (1898), a trooper of the 21st Lancers and his horse find themselves in a thirsty situation. During this campaign the Anglo-Egyptian forces under Sir Horatio Kitchener were fighting the Khalifa's Dervish army which had maintained an iron grip on the Sudan since the death of General Gordon 13 years earlier. The model is 54 mm (2in), the more common commercial size. (R. Hailes)

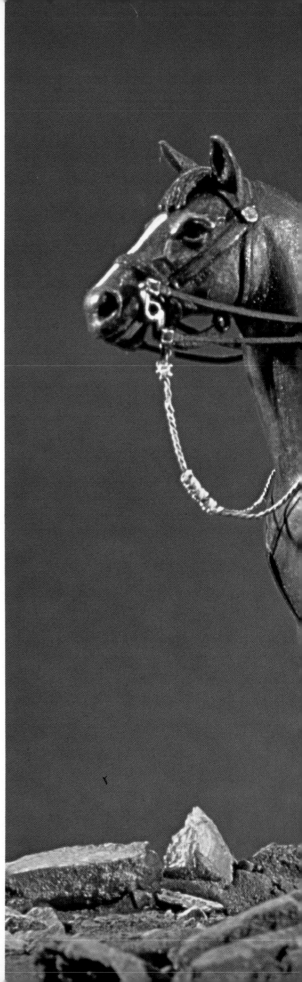

South Africa in 1879 was the background to one of the bitterest and most fiercely fought wars ever undertaken by the British Army. The Zulu nation inhabited a large tract of land to the north of Durban, and, under successive kings, had developed into a strict military regime. The entire male population from adolescence to late middle age was liable for service and was formed into regiments, each containing the men of a particular age group and having its own costume. As further identification, shield colours also related to regimental age categories, ranging from the black hides used for 'young' units to the almost total white of the royal guard. Every regiment had its title, jealously upheld, and was commanded by an *induna*. The Zulu army dealt the British some shrewd knocks before its final defeat at Ulundi. The regimental *induna* (*above*) is armed with the deadly stabbing assegai. (Realmodels; K. Butt)

Another Indian Army cavalry piece is pictured (*right*); it represents the Risaldar Major of the 18th Tiwana Lancers. (J. Runnicles)

MODERN CONFLICTS

Dominated by the events of two world wars, the 20th century has witnessed the introduction of weapons and equipment of increasing complexity and effect, which still, however, need men to operate and maintain them, like this British signals linesman in World War I. (DEK Models)

The Great War of 1914–18 was the first in which the whole world became involved; even a few neutral countries were forced to mobilize their men so that their neutrality would be respected by all the warring nations. Most of the significant land battles took place in Europe where enormous armies battered one another for years trying to achieve some sort of result. In the West, after the first few weeks of movement, fighting deteriorated into a stalemate in which French, British and German troops crouched in opposing trench systems which stretched unbroken from the Channel coast to the Swiss border. Neither side could break out of this deadlock despite the huge numbers of men, bullets, shells and missiles that were brought to bear. Casualties mounted enormously in set-piece attacks against positions that were almost impossible to take, over ground churned up by explosives into a mass of thick mud in which men, animals and machines could disappear without trace. Movement of wheeled vehicles on the battlefield therefore became impossible and light railways were built to ease transportation of those loads that could not be carried on the backs of horses, mules or men.

In this diorama (*below*), wounded soldiers are being taken to the rear by light railway. The railway is powered by German prisoners escorted by a Tommy (British soldier) with fixed bayonet. The

iece is very successful in conveying the sombre
mosphere of the Western Front. (R. Philpott)

All Allied troops in this area were under the
erall supreme command of the French General,
er Marshal, Foch (*top right*). This model is
geniously constructed with parts from a number
plastic assembly kits and some oddments of scrap
astic. (D. Hunter)

The Russian infantryman (*bottom right*) is rep-
sentative of the gigantic army deployed on the
stern Front. Badly commanded, the Russians
perienced several major defeats including the early
saster at Tannenberg. Low in morale, they col-
osed into revolution in 1917. (John Tassel)

World War II began with the invasion of Poland, then settled into a period of stagnation. This ended abruptly in 1940 with the German *blitzkrieg* campaign, swift defeat for France and the aerial onslaught known as the Battle of Britain. Won decisively by the RAF, the outcome of the battle enabled the British to re-equip and undertake the series of campaigns, alone and with allies, that were to end in total victory some five years later. An RAF pilot (*right*), returned from an interception mission, shows with appropriate gestures how he dealt with the enemy. His informal dress is typical of that worn against regulations but developed as a style by fighter pilots. (WMH Models)

A German amphibious Schwimmwagen emerges from the water on the Russian Front (*below*) in an excellent example of how figures can combine harmoniously with vehicle subjects, to the advantage of both. (Donald Skinner)

General Alexander (*far right*) held command in the United Kingdom, Far East and the desert before becoming Allied Supremo in the Italian campaign, and later important as a diplomat and politician. The figure shows 'Alex', map in hand, issuing orders to his subordinate commanders. (David Hunter)

A Japanese sniper is here pictured (*right*) during the Burma campaigns of 1943–5. The Japanese adapted their training and tactics very successfully to jungle warfare, enjoying considerable early victories, but eventually, Allied troops became just as expert in close country, and with better supplies were driving them back even before the explosion of atom bombs over Japan abruptly ended the war in August 1945. (D. Skinner)

A British Land Rover ambulance (*below*) is posed against a Northern Ireland background. The vehicle and its accompanying soldier figures are accurate in all the details of finish, uniform and equipment. Since 1969, service in Ulster has taken on the aspect of actual campaigning with real bullets being fired and casualties being incurred, even among the civilian population in many areas. (D. Skinner)

Another facet of contemporary war is depict (*below right*) by an Angolan MPLA soldier runni through the bush in southwest Africa. The figure made by the conversion process applied to pa taken from the splendid Multipose assembly ki manufactured in plastic by Airfix Ltd. By ringi the changes between various sets in this series, surprising number of different attitudes can achieved. This model is carrying a Russian weapo (The independence battle in Angola involved t great powers who gave support to both sides.) Thi a good example of how attention to detail, bc physical and historical, is an essential part of being successful modeller. (R. Smith)

On *page 64* is a German motorcycle combinati used in World War II reconnaissance units. It jo a superbly detailed plastic kit with magnifice scratchbuilt figures. (W. Hearne)

INDEX

Acknowledgements
All photographs by John Wylie, ex
following by Roy Dilley: 6, 44 belo

**First published 1981 by
Octopus Books Limited
59 Grosvenor Street
London W1**

ISBN 0 7064 1432.2

© 1981 Octopus Books Limited

Produced by
Mandarin Publishers Limited
22a Westlands Road,
Quarry Bay, Hong Kong

Printed in Hong Kong